MIKE YC

SUPERTED AND THE HELICOPTER PIRATES

Illustrations by Philip Watkins

FREDERICK MULLER LIMITED
LONDON.

The headline in the newspaper worried Superted. He read 'Helicopter Pirates Strike Again. Six-year-old son of television star kidnapped.'

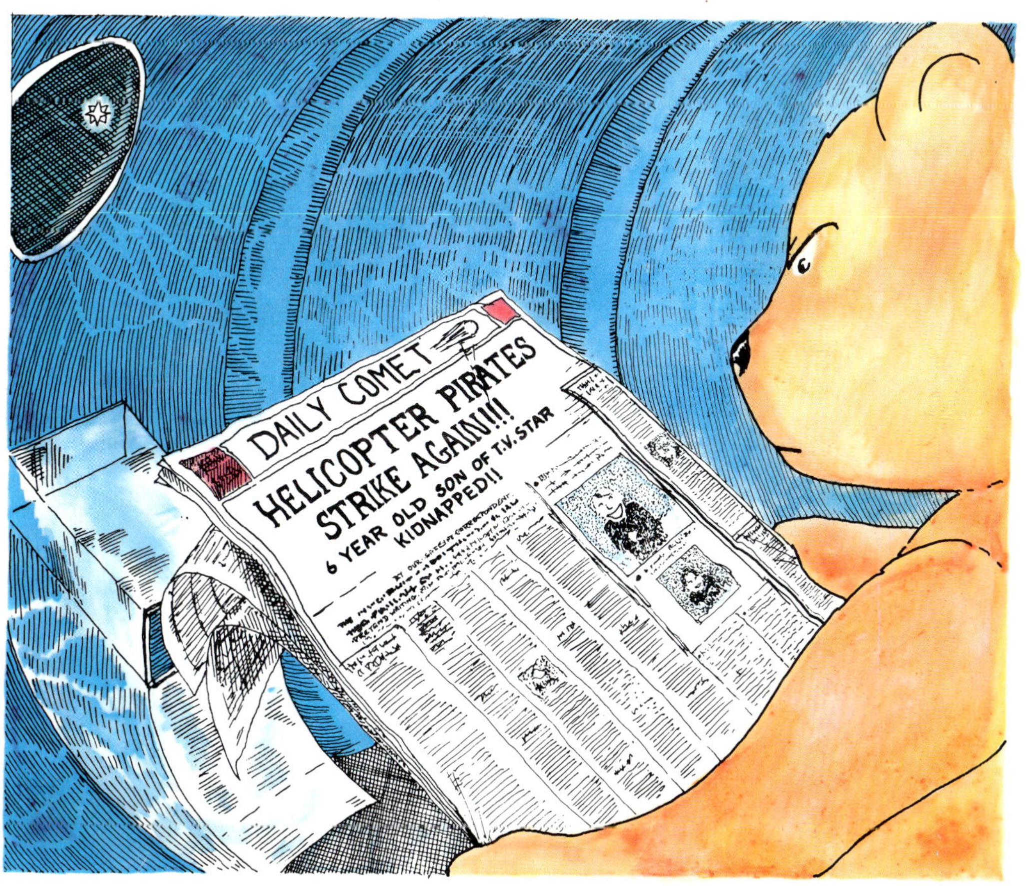
DAILY COMET
HELICOPTER PIRATES STRIKE AGAIN!!!
6 YEAR OLD SON OF T.V. STAR KIDNAPPED!!

The helicopter pirates were very daring. Only last month they had flown their large red helicopter over a security van containing lots of money and had snatched it up by using a claw-like grab. Just last week they had stolen all the parcels from a mail train. Two of the three pirates had climbed down a rope-ladder suspended from the helicopter, on to the roof of the speeding train. They had made the engine-driver stop the train by frightening him with their pirates' cutlasses.

SECURE

Superted now read that yesterday they had kidnapped Richard, the son of a famous television star, by landing their helicopter in a children's playground. They had then bundled the little boy into their helicopter while his frightened playmates looked on helplessly.

Superted switched on his video scanners and soon spotted the helicopter pirates' hideaway. It was a pirate sailing-ship anchored beside a secret island in the middle of the ocean.

Superted whispered his very special magic word, and in a jiff had turned from an ordinary ted into Superted.

He then flew out of his space-station home determined to capture the helicopter pirates' hideout and to save Richard.

MAXIMUM ZOOM

Soon Superted was flying over the pirate ship.

One of the pirates spotted him. 'Man the cannon, shipmates,' he shouted.

The pirates shot their largest cannonball at Superted, who easily dodged it. 'You pirates had better let Richard go or you'll be sorry,' he yelled.

One of the nastiest-looking pirates stood Richard on a wooden plank jutting out over the sea and said, 'If you don't go away we'll push the boy over the side.'

Superted did not trust the pirate, and only pretended to fly away. In fact he hid in a small cloud nearby.

When the pirate thought Superted had gone, he said in his pirate's growl, 'Over the side you go, me Bucko. It's getting too dangerous for us here with Superted around.' With that he pushed Richard, who started to fall towards the water, where there was a large shark waiting for his dinner.

In a flash Superted flew down and caught the little boy just in time.

The pirates jumped into their helicopter and took off. Superted put Richard on the deck of the pirate ship and flew after them at top speed, soon chasing them high up in the sky. One of the pirates threw a large net out of the open door of the helicopter and Superted became terribly tangled up and started to fall towards the sea. Faster and faster he fell.

'Hee! Hee!' laughed the wicked pirates.

Splash! Into the sea fell Superted. Down under the water he sank.

Holding his breath and opening his eyes, he saw a sharp underwater rock. Then, using his great strength, he ripped a hole in the net—and whoosh! At super underwater speed he rocketed upwards, out of the sea and into the sky.

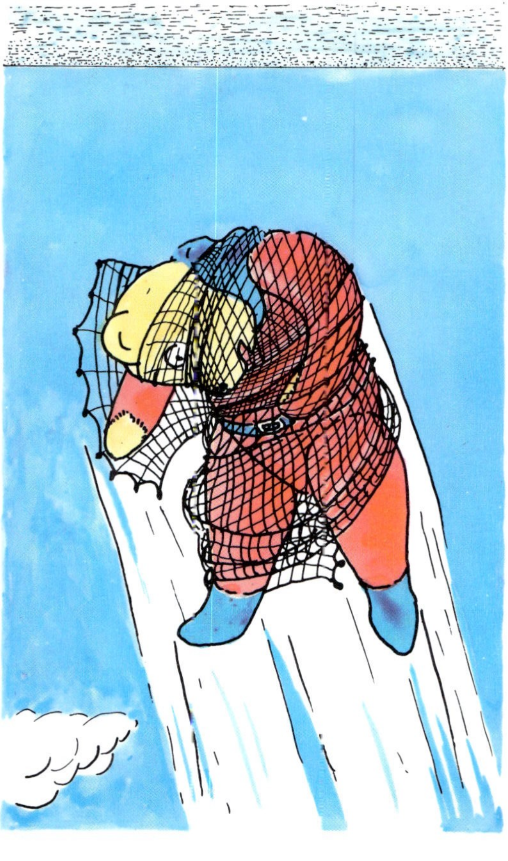

The pirates had thought they had got away, but in seconds Superted was up with them again.

He caught hold of the helicopter rotor-blades, tied them into a knot, and shook the helicopter until all the pirates fell out.

Superted said, 'I am going to put you on a secret desert island, where you will teach yourselves to be good sailors. I shall come back from time to time to make sure you do.'

The next day Superted was reading his newspaper again—but this time there was a photograph of him being presented with a special bravery award by Richard's father.

Good old Superted.

DAILY COMET
GOOD OLD SUPERTED!!!